YOUR KNOWLEDGE HAS VALUE

- We will publish your bachelor's and master's thesis, essays and papers

- Your own eBook and book - sold worldwide in all relevant shops

- Earn money with each sale

Upload your text at www.GRIN.com
and publish for free

Bibliographic information published by the German National Library:

The German National Library lists this publication in the National Bibliography; detailed bibliographic data are available on the Internet at http://dnb.dnb.de .

This book is copyright material and must not be copied, reproduced, transferred, distributed, leased, licensed or publicly performed or used in any way except as specifically permitted in writing by the publishers, as allowed under the terms and conditions under which it was purchased or as strictly permitted by applicable copyright law. Any unauthorized distribution or use of this text may be a direct infringement of the author s and publisher s rights and those responsible may be liable in law accordingly.

Imprint:

Copyright © 2015 GRIN Verlag
Print and binding: Books on Demand GmbH, Norderstedt Germany
ISBN: 9783668642522

This book at GRIN:

https://www.grin.com/document/413350

Jobaire Alam

What has research shown about the effects of terrorism and other dramatic events on subjective risk judgments, worries and travel desire?

GRIN Verlag

GRIN - Your knowledge has value

Since its foundation in 1998, GRIN has specialized in publishing academic texts by students, college teachers and other academics as e-book and printed book. The website www.grin.com is an ideal platform for presenting term papers, final papers, scientific essays, dissertations and specialist books.

Visit us on the internet:

http://www.grin.com/

http://www.facebook.com/grincom

http://www.twitter.com/grin_com

University of Stavanger

Norwegian School of Hotel Management

MSc in International Hotel & Tourism Leadership

Final Exam Individual

MHR 175: Psychology; Employee and Customer Experiences

Title: What has research shown about the effects of terrorism and other dramatic events on subjective risk judgments, worries and travel desire?

Introduction

The discussion topic "What has research shown about the effects of terrorism and other dramatic events on subjective risk judgments, worries and travel desire?" is a question of tourism social psychology. As terrorism is a threat for every individual issue, so it has a massive impact on tourism society. Again worry is a combination of fear and anxiety (S. Larsen, Brun, W., & Ogaard, T., 2009), therefore because of terrorist attacks and other dramatic events tourist minds become worried about safety. The tourists may start to consider about the risk factors of travelling to a particular destination and thus the willingness of touring might be affected too. By the support and assistance of the current researches, I would like to define the key terms. Then I would like to describe what the current researches have shown about the impact of terrorism and other dramatic events on subjective risk judgments, worries and travel desire.

Defining Terrorism and other dramatic events

Walter and Todd on the fifth page of their book 'The Political Economy of Terrorism' have defined terrorism alternatively 'as a premeditative violence which has got political motivation' (Enders, 2006). They further added '…This violence is again sudden occurrence against the civilians, targeted by other national groups or clandestine agents, generally to influence a society by establishing an instance sometimes in order to implement their rights, demands and sometimes not.' (Enders, 2006). Terrorism does not happen always by the political motivation. It has lots of other social motivations too. Because of these contingent events the terrorist groups make genocide by the revengeful attempts from their perspective. So therefore, all the terrorist attacks are dramatic and sudden events. There are some other sudden and unexpected events what can make the tourist society worry about traveling to a specific destination, for example natural devastation, massive destruction by political instability, pestilence in some countries or areas etc. All these sudden and dramatic contingencies have really a massive impact on tourists mind. As a result, the tourist groups may take into consideration about some risk factors and become worry about the trip. (S. Larsen, Brun, W., & Ogaard, T., 2009).

Defining subjective risk judgment, worries and travel desire

Subjective risk judgment:

According to Holmberg, 2002; Lepp & Gibson, 2003; Callander & Page, 2003, as cited in the research article of (S. Larsen, Brun, W., Ogaard, T., & Selstad, L., 2011),

> '...within the tourism literature research scholars have focused on the risk factors which are related to travelling. Those risk factors are for example health risk, political instability, terrorism, strange food, cultural barriers, crime and a nation's political and religious dogma. Moreover the risks, which are connected to the adventure tourism, risk narratives in backpackers, subjective risk in backpackers, rationalizations of such risks, drug use, construction of certain areas as risky, food risk (S. Larsen, Brun, W., Øgaard, T., & Selstad, L., 2007) and tourists' worries (S. Larsen, Brun, W., & Ogaard, T., 2009).'

According to Wikipedia definition, the risk perception is mental judgment which establishes the traits and seriousness of the risk. This is generally used in reference usual obstacles and threats to the environment or health. The idea subjective risk has a various practices in the social psychological science which has multidimensional concepts ("Risk Perception," 2013).

Worry:

An understandable and proper definition of worry has been found from the research article of Svein, Wibecke & Torvald, 2009 that "The concept of worry is related to fear and anxiety and to other aspects of psychological health, worry seems to be a more important issue in psychology than in the general study of tourists and tourism…" They added by saying, "Worry may be understood as negative affect and relatively uncontrollable chains of thought as a function of uncertainty concerning possible future events." (S. Larsen, Brun, W., & Ogaard, T., 2009).

Furthermore, from the words of Borkovec, 1994; Borkovec, Robinson, Pruzinsky, & DePree, 1983; Borkovec and Inz 1990, as it has been cited in the same research article, "Such thoughts are viewed as representing the individuals' attempts to engage in mental problem solving on issues where the outcome is uncertain but contains a possibility for negative results." Moreover, "Although worry is related to anxiety and depression, worry is still, as opposed to anxiety and depression, predominantly a cognitive activity involving what label verbal-linguistic thinking." (S. Larsen, Brun, W., & Ogaard, T., 2009).

Travel desire:

According to the words of Passer & Smith, 2003, p. 327; Dann, 1997, 1981; Gyimothy & Mykletun, 2004; Iso-Ahola, 1982; McCabe, 2000; what have been cited in the empirical research paper of Svein, Wibecke, Torvald & Leif in 2011, 'The "travel desire" variable is not to be confused with concepts of motivation in general, which is often conceptualized as a process that gives direction, intensity and persistence to goal-directed behaviors.' They further explained that the motivation of tourist is often understood as escaping from the regularity of life. In that research paper, travel desire only represented the lust expression of individual, or desire to make a specific type of trip to a particular destination without any restraint. (S. Larsen, Brun, W., Ogaard, T., & Selstad, L., 2011).

Discussion on effects of terrorism and other dramatic events on risk judgments, worries and travel desire; what researches have shown us

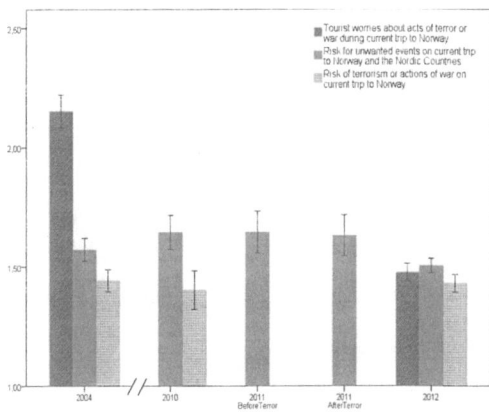

Risk Perception

The chart on left is indicating the worries and risk judgments of tourists in Norway before-after the massacre events of 2011 at Utoya, Oslo. Here the mean values on a scale from 1-7. The chart and the data have been found and taken directly from the research about 'Risk Perception and Worries' of Professor Svein and Katharina (Wolff, in press).

The researchers wanted to clarify by the empirical study; if terrorism could make the tourists feel safer. In order to do that, the professors have taken the incident of 22nd July 2011 at Utoya, Oslo. The research was about short and long term risk perceptions among tourists. According to their finding as directly taken from (Wolff, in press), "Our findings are in stark contrast to earlier research regarding the effect of terrorism on the tourism industry and on risk perceptions of tourists." They found a decreasing number of visiting tourists, temporary increase in perceived risk because of a terror attack. The study however indicated a decline in risk perceptions and worries following the 2011 Oslo/Utoya massacre. "…Since these findings are novel and unexpected future research will have to look into how these terror attacks differ from other calamities studied in the field. One possible difference is baseline risk perceptions regarding a destination." Moreover, they added, the destinations which are generally ridden by terrorism and where the attacks are committed by non-organized individuals the risk perception increases and decreases respectively. (Wolff, in press).

The findings of another research article by Myron, Heather, Lori & Brijesh 2008; in the 'Journal of Travel and Tourism marketing' is indicating risk perception of tourists, were consistent with previous literature of Roehl and Fesenmaier, 1992; which has been cited in that article. In their own words, the aim of this study was to experiment the influence of perceived risk on travel intentions in the aftermath of the 09/11 events. "The sample, consisting of households from the N.Y area, is significant because of its proximity to "Ground Zero" and because of its importance as the leading designated market area in the U.S.' (Floyd, 2008). These events provides opportunity to study overall behavior of tourists in terms of risk, worries & desire. That study implied three factors associated with perceived risk towards travel. Among the three factors, travel risk got the strongest level of agreement. That's why risk perception was given individual attention in the survey of this study. (Floyd, 2008). In order to examine the risk perception, "Travel experience emerged as the most significant predictor of travel intentions. This result is consistent with previous research which suggests that past experience might override one's perception of risk." (Floyd, 2008).

Tourist Worries

In order to explore the stability and sensitivity of the Tourist Worry Scale in terms of tourists' real life incidents of terrorism, Wibecke, Katharina & Svein 2011; conducted the research on tourist worries after terrorist attack. Their results confirmed that,

> "…..a large majority of the respondents agreed that the world as such as well as popular tourist destinations had become more dangerous after the "War on terror" was launched, with a significant increase in ratings from pre to post-terror measurement. Interestingly, the results showed that the overall TWS ratings were stable over the months from before to after the serious terrorist attacks during the summer of 2005. Even more interesting is that the single item measuring worries concerning terror, was indeed sensitive to the heightened risk due to the outburst of terrorist attacks, as a significant change in worry concerning terror was found. However, despite a significant increase, average rating of worry related to terrorism still remained low." (Brun, 2011).

Travel Desire

The research of Svein, Wibecke, Torvald & Leif derived that '…change in peoples' overall risk judgments concerning travel destinations as a consequence of the war, but that the war gave a temporarily negative effect on people's desire to travel…'(S. Larsen, Brun, W., Ogaard, T., & Selstad, L., 2011). They farther found that travel desire and risk judgments are relevant to many other holiday forms which have been converted over since the end of April 2004. (S. Larsen, Brun, W., Ogaard, T., & Selstad, L., 2011).

Conclusion

After studying several researches which have been conducted over last few years by Svein, Wibecke, Torvald, Leif, Katharina, Myron, Heather, Lori & Brijesh it would not be easy to draw a conclusion on the discussion topic. According to their tourism psychological researches, nevertheless, no study could retrieve that whether the decision making related to travel choices of the tourist is depending on emotional reaction. By the words of Wibecke, Katharina & Svein, "We conclude that several aspects of the dynamics and interactions of affective states and travel choices in situations of heightened risk are still "virgin soil" in the tourism domain, waiting to be explored." (Brun, 2011). They suggested for the future researches to find out more promising results for improvement in the tourism sector and in the tourist society. (S. Larsen, Brun, W., & Ogaard, T., 2009).

Reference

Brun, W., Wolff, K., & Larsen, S. (2011). Tourist Worries after Terrorist Attacks: Report from a Field Experiment. *Scandinavian Journal of Hospitality and Tourism, 11*(3), 387-394.

Enders, W., & Sandler, T. (2006). *The Political Economy of Terrorism* Retrieved from http://www.google.no/books?hl=no&lr=&id=9JS7pKPHqlIC&oi=fnd&pg=PP1&dq=Direct+Definition+of+Terrorism+and+other+dramatic+events&ots=caeK8YVmGc&sig=HcptKKqlvw645pcFSDQxsWGJPW4&redir_esc=y#v=onepage&q&f=false

Floyd, M. F., Gibson, H., Pennington-Gray, L., & Thapa, B. (2008). The Effect of Risk Perceptions on Intentions to Travel in the Aftermath of September 11, 2001. *Journal of Travel and Tourism Marketing, 15*(2-3), 19-38. http://dx.doi.org/10.1300/J073v15n02_02

Larsen, S., Brun, W., & Ogaard, T. (2009). What tourists worry about – construction of a scale measuring tourist worries. *Tourism Management, 30*, 260-265.

Larsen, S., Brun, W., Ogaard, T., & Selstad, L. (2011). Effects of Sudden and Dramatic Events on Travel Desire and Risk Judgements. *Scandinavian Journal of Hospitality and Tourism, 11*(3), 268-285.

http://www.tandfonline.com/doi/abs/10.1080/15022250.2011.593360#.UqXFWtJDuRY

Larsen, S., Brun, W., Øgaard, T., & Selstad, L. (2007). Subjective food-risk judgments in tourists. *Tourism Management, 28*(6), 1555-1559.

Risk Perception. (2013). Retrieved 10/12/2013, from

http://en.wikipedia.org/wiki/Risk_perception

Wolff, K., & Larsen, S. (in press). Can terrorism make us feel safer? Risk Perceptions and Worries Before and After the July 22nd Attacks. . *Annals of Tourism Research.*

YOUR KNOWLEDGE HAS VALUE

- We will publish your bachelor's and master's thesis, essays and papers

- Your own eBook and book - sold worldwide in all relevant shops

- Earn money with each sale

Upload your text at www.GRIN.com
and publish for free